How to Raise Monarch Butterflies

For Children with Adults

By
Mary-Elin Renzullo
Text © 2012

Edited 2019
Illustrator, photographer, and designer: Coco Tse

Thanks to Jim Lovett, Research Assistant, of Monarch Watch (monarchwatch.org)
for the picture on page 24 of the "swarm" of Monarchs in Mexico.

Table of Contents

Life Cycle of a Monarch Butterfly

Introduction

Raising Monarch butterflies is one of the great joys of summer. Most of all, it's lots of fun. Yes, it is educational too, but it's more than that. It illustrates the beauty of nature. Watching this hungry caterpillar grow, day by day, from barely a spot on a leaf, to being 2 inches long, is amazing! When this creature sheds its skin for the last time, the bright bands of yellow and black are no longer needed. The milky green body inside slowly hardens to form its chrysalis. It's hard to believe this is happening right in front of your eyes! Now it's time to wait and watch for a while. Eventually, the Monarch emerges from its chrysalis, pumps up its wings and body, rests and dries. When it finally flies away, its extraordinary life cycle begins once more.

I have raised monarchs for over 50 years and have learned a great deal from my experiences. Also, there are many books written about this subject, both nonfiction and fiction, so you can get specific information from books in any library, and of course, online. I have read many of these books, but this booklet will focus on my personal observations and tips for success. So, although writers are told to avoid the word "I" as much as possible, you will find plenty of "I, I, I's" in this booklet.

If you have any questions, I will be glad to help. Let me know how you make out. I would love to hear from you. Email me at **mary-elin@hotmail.com** or call me at home (860) 379-1438.

Milkweed

This plant is the beginning of it all. The butterfly lays its eggs on the underside of this leaf, caterpillars eat <u>only</u> milkweed, and often, they place their chrysalis on, or very close to, this plant. Luckily, there is plenty of it around. I just learned from www.monarchwatch.com that there are over 100 kinds of milkweed. The milky white substance inside the plant will make the butterfly poisonous and bad tasting to its enemies.

Milkweed is common along the sides of the roads or open fields where it can receive sun, I have even found it in little dirt patches outside malls and other unlikely places, so keep your eyes open for it in June, July, and August.

This photo shows the kind found in this area, but you won't see these flowers when you are hunting for caterpillars in July. They will be gone by then. Look for your milkweed supply in June and the flowers may be present then. I have tried uprooting the whole plant and putting it in water. Sometimes it works, sometimes it doesn't. Most often, I pick off the leaves, at the main stem, enough for a few days' supply of food for my hungry caterpillars at home, and put those in a cup with a little water in the bottom. They will last for several days.

Do not mistake Dogbane for milkweed. They look very much alike, but Dogbane has much softer leaves, and is generally smaller. The caterpillars may taste it a little, but will die if they continue to eat it.

Growing Milkweed

I usually grow milkweed in my yard (although my husband complains a lot). It's very convenient for feeding, but also, Monarchs may lay their eggs on your plants. To plant your own milkweed, wait until the Fall when the pods are crusty and full of seeds with fluffy "parachutes". Then, simply imitate Mother Nature. Spread the seeds where you want them to grow, and sprinkle them with a bit of dirt, just enough to keep them in your yard. Probably the rain, wind, and snow will plant them in the earth at the proper depth. In the Spring, some will sprout and each year they will multiply.

It may be a good idea to cut back some of your plants, just like the street crews mow the roadsides. I used to get angry when they did that, thinking of all the creatures they have killed (actually, it still makes me sad). But I've discovered that on the sides of the road, some plants will grow again and you will still have fresh leaves later in the season. I've never really trimmed my own milkweed, but I may try it, maybe one or two plants at first.

Lately I have been transplanting milkweed plants I find in the wild to my own yard when I know it's a location where the milkweed will just be cut down anyway. I use a shovel and dig up as much dirt around the plant and try to save as much root as possible.

The Egg

At first it may be difficult for you to find an egg because they are so small. I have brought home many aphids, thinking they were eggs. Actually, eggs are smaller than aphids, and of course, they won't disappear like an aphid will. The egg is always found on the underside of the milkweed leaves, laid there by the butterfly to shade them from the sun. You have to turn over every leaf carefully to check out the underside, looking for something white and pointed. If you do find one, pick the whole leaf, at the stem, and at home, place it upright against the side of a jar with a bit of water in the bottom, to keep the leaf alive until the egg hatches in a day or two. The caterpillar that hatches is so small it looks like a teeny black line. It will eat the eggshell first, and then will start on the leaf. In fact, one good way to find a newly hatched caterpillar is to look for a leaf that has a very small hole eaten out of it. Then you will know the egg has hatched, and the caterpillar may still be underneath, near the hole.

This greatly enlarged picture is of an egg. When it has a black tip, which is the caterpillar inside, it means it is ready to hatch. Most eggs that you find will probably be just white.

Occasionally you may be lucky enough to see a Monarch butterfly alight on the edge of a leaf and lay its egg on the underside. It's happened to me!

5

Caterpillars

The Monarch caterpillar is quite distinctive with its black, yellow and white stripes. Its size can be very small, almost invisible, up to about 2 inches. The only other caterpillar that you might get confused with (at first) is the one that has colors somewhat similar to the Monarch caterpillar, but has long hairs sticking up all over its body, like a Mohawk haircut. Plus, I think it's somewhat ugly compared to the sleek and colorful body of the Monarch caterpillar. Anyway, it's also on the milkweed.

You already know that the newborn caterpillars are most often found on the underside of the leaves, and so are the larger ones. However, you might find the bigger fellows on top of the leaves or on the stems, so it's necessary to look over the whole milkweed plant. If you see a big part of a leaf missing, that might mean a large caterpillar is nearby. When you find one, pick the whole leaf and try not to touch the caterpillar or bother it. If your new friend doesn't like what you're doing, it will raise up its head and kind of wave it around, as if to say "Hey you, leave me alone!" (You can tell the head from the back end because the front filaments are longer than the rear ones. They are not antennae). If the caterpillar is on a stem or somewhere else, pick a leaf and gently slide it under its front "feet". It may object to this but keep at it, gently. It will probably figure out what you are doing and walk (slowly…slowly) onto the leaf for you. Then you can get it home safely without upsetting it any more.

The search for eggs and caterpillars begins in mid-July through August. The weather contributes to how many there are to find.

Too hot, too rainy, too cold = fewer caterpillars.

Here are a few different sized Monarch caterpillars. I would never put a big one in the same jar with a tiny one, though. Believe it or not, the larger fellow may eat the little guy. It's happened to me. Each caterpillar should have its own jar. That solves all the problems, like fighting over food or eating someone else. Also, every chrysalis will emerge on its own schedule, and you don't want anything to be in the way during that process.

The Chrysalis

When the caterpillar is about 2 inches, it will be time for it to shed its skin for the last time and create the chrysalis. How do you know when this is about to happen? The caterpillar will stop eating, crawl to the top of the jar, hopefully to the netting, and begin to spin a little mat of silk. Next, comes a silk knob on the mat called a "button". When all that work is complete, it will hang, head first, from the button, and will curl up the head part to form a "J" shape. Books say this hanging around lasts a few hours, but I have seen it last much longer than that, even overnight. When the filaments on the head begin to sag, looking as if they will fall off, and the body looks greenish under the skin of the caterpillar, you can be sure that the process will begin very soon.

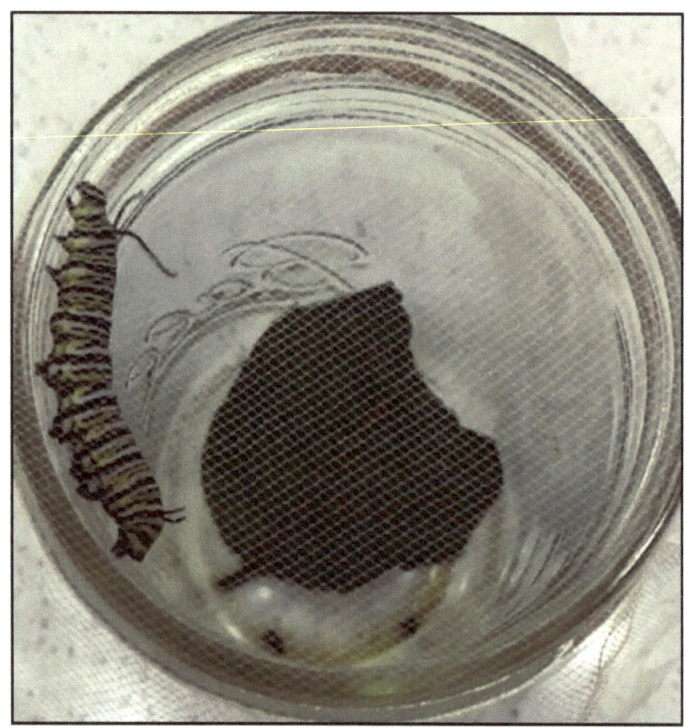

Once the caterpillar has formed a "J" shape, its body becomes more greenish, which is the body inside showing through the skin. Another thing to look at are the filaments on the head. They will be hanging down, looking like they are ready to fall off. That's because they <u>are</u> ready to fall off, along with the rest of the skin! When you see that, it won't be long before the skin will split. I wouldn't go shopping right now, or go to bed, if you want to see it happen!

The creation of the chrysalis begins when the outer skin of black, yellow and white stripes splits at the back of the head and continues to split up the back. This skin shrinks and balls up at the top where it is attached to the button. The caterpillar squirms and twists to get the skin off. I'm always afraid it will fall off its little attachment, but it never has. When the ball of skin has fallen to the bottom of the jar, the caterpillar will be all green and will still twist around a bit. Soon it will stop, and an outside layer of the green body will harden into the chrysalis. Try not to jostle either the caterpillar or the chrysalis, and be sure to **keep your beautiful chrysalis out of direct sunlight!** Although it is a beautiful green color, that is the pupa inside. The chrysalis has just a very thin clear crust, as you will see after the butterfly emerges. It has what seem like golden dots for decoration! Scientists are still working on what the golden dots are for.

11

The Butterfly

The caterpillar inside the chrysalis is now called the pupa. For about 10 days, many changes take place inside this shiny green creation. One day, you will see that it has turned black. (At first, I was afraid it had rotted). The next day it will be clear and you will be able to see the orange and black wings of the butterfly inside. This is the day that the butterfly will emerge from its chrysalis. Keep a close watch on it. Also, I hate to tell you this, but many of mine have come out at night when no one is around. I think they prefer darkness and complete silence. I suppose darkness might be safer in the wild, because it takes a good two hours for the wings to dry, and even a bit longer before it is interested in flying away.

Sometimes the ball of skin does not successfully fall off the chrysalis, but it has never hurt the formation of the butterfly inside, in my experience.

As soon as the butterfly comes out, it will hang from the empty chrysalis, which always seems pretty precarious to me. If it ends up grasping the netting, that seems safer to me. Immediately, it will begin to pump up its wings with a special fluid. This only takes about five minutes. If it should fall during this process, it will not be able to finish pumping up its wings. It will die eventually, because it will not be able to fly. Sad, but true. I've tried to save a few when they've fallen, but always unsuccessfully. It's amazing to see this emergence, but again, do not jostle the Monarch during this time.

Butterfly Anatomy

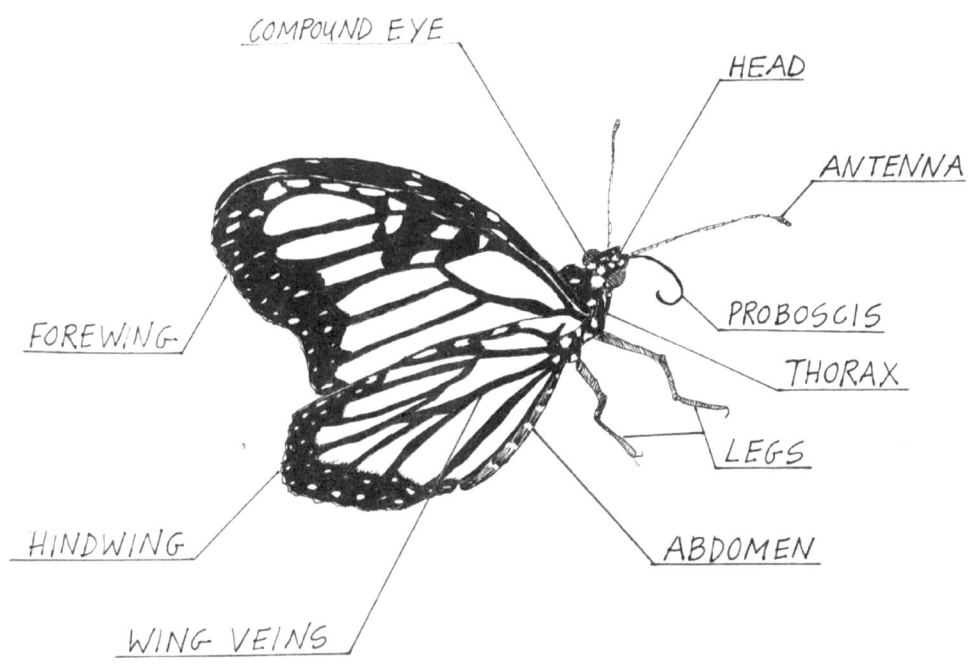

COMPOUND EYE

HEAD

ANTENNA

FOREWING

PROBOSCIS

THORAX

LEGS

HINDWING

ABDOMEN

WING VEINS

Releasing Your Butterfly

After the wings are nice and plump, the butterfly rests for a few hours as the wings dry completely. I have found that even after that, it is not interested in flying away. I give it at least five hours before I set it free. It can even stay overnight in the jar if you wish (it will practice flapping its wings). It won't die of hunger overnight, so do not worry about feeding it.

I always want to know if my butterfly is a boy or girl. This is very easy to tell. The picture above is a boy (a male) because it has a dot on each of the wings closest to the body. A female has no dots, shown on the next page. Before you let it go, take a look at the wings. I used to name all my boys Michael, and the girls either Elizabeth or Catherine (my children). Now I name them Holly, Parker, Grayson and Tristan, my grandchildren!

Watching your gorgeous Monarch fly away – up, up, up into the sky, is an exciting experience. To release it, go outside first and remove the netting (You don't need a butterfly in your house!). If the butterfly is clinging to the jar, or on the bottom and refuses to come out, gently and slowly place your finger under the front legs, and it will crawl on. It won't hurt you, of course, but watch out – it tickles. <u>It won't fly away in the rain, and it will not fly at temperatures lower than 50°.</u> It's not crazy about 60° either. If you have a late hatching, such as later in September, you may have a problem with colder temperatures. If I need to go to work, and the little critter will not fly away, I set the opened jar on my steps, and it decides when it is ready to leave home. When I come home, my jar is always empty. Or I'll take it to school and set it free with one of my classes.

Care and Feeding

Finding a Proper Jar- Before you begin searching for caterpillars, you should start collecting glass jars (plastic is okay, but you can see through glass better). The opening needs to be large enough to fit your hand through, and it should be over 4 inches tall so the Monarch will have plenty of room when it emerges. The top will be covered by a piece of netting (sized larger than the top) held on by an elastic.

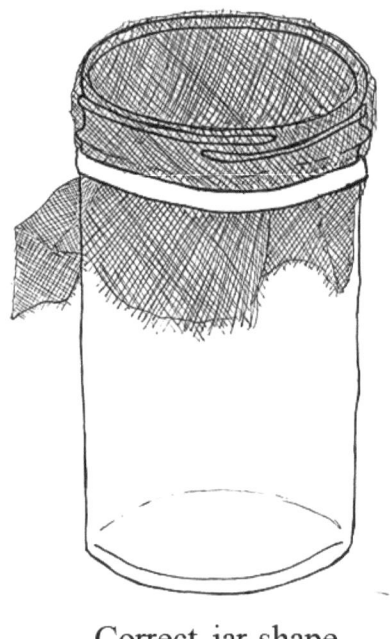

Correct jar shape

Also, punching holes in a lid, as the picture below suggests, creates sharp edges. Caterpillars seem very curious to me and will crawl anywhere! Ouch! Use netting with very small holes, because they are escape artists, even when they are very little, and when you least expect it.

This jar shape below is not the best choice. The caterpillar often makes its chrysalis where the arrows show. It may emerge too close to the side of the jar, and then, there may not be enough room for the new butterfly to pump up its wings. A jar with straight sides is best, as shown before, because the butterfly is forced to make its chrysalis on the netting covering the top. The netting also gives the new butterfly another place to grip as it dries. Normally, it will hold on to its empty chrysalis while it does a swaying, twisting motion, part of the whole process.

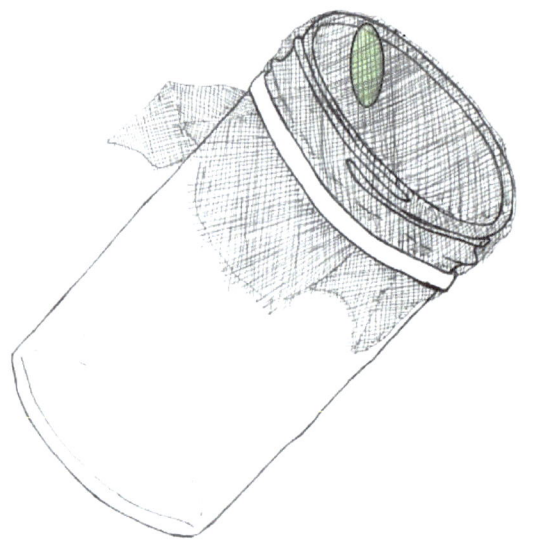

If the caterpillar makes its chrysalis in a bad spot, I tilt the jar (when the chrysalis is completely dry) to help the butterfly when it comes out, from being too close to the side of the jar. Figure out some way to prop the jar in this position, securely, until the butterfly leaves home.

Now to the feeding of your caterpillar – when you put a leaf into the jar, overlap one end of the leaf outside the rim of the jar (to prevent it from sagging as the larger size caterpillars chomp on it). Place the netting over the top of the jar, holding it in place with an elastic. Make sure it holds the leaf in place, and has no open spots (where the elastic might not be holding the netting). If there are any holes where a caterpillar can crawl out, it probably will. I don't know why, since it has a perfectly good leaf to munch on, but I have had many caterpillars escape over the years! Usually I find the little devils, but I have also found chrysalises under my counters and under my kitchen chairs, so I know for sure I didn't find all of my escapees!

If you find that your little buddy is a really active crawler, be sure the netting on top is the kind with very, very tiny holes. Sometimes I even use a thin flimsy material from one of my daughter's old ballet costumes. Air passes through, but no caterpillar, no matter how small could get out. Of course, I guarantee nothing – these are tricky little creatures!

One of the most important things to remember is to keep your caterpillars and chrysalises **out of the sunshine**. In nature, caterpillars stay in the shade most of the time, and would never put their chrysalis where the sun could melt it.

It's OK to have more than one caterpillar in a jar when they are small, but when they get big, they should each have their own jar to make the chrysalis. When they emerge, it is not a good idea to disturb one chrysalis which is attached to the netting in order to free another butterfly in the same jar that wants to fly away.

If you see a caterpillar not eating, or moving very little, don't be worried. It is probably shedding its skin, which happens four or five times. For some of these fellows, it can take a day or two, and it seems to take a lot of effort. When it's done, it will begin to eat again. You may even be able to see the shed skin on the bottom of the jar, in a little ball with the filaments sticking out.

Caterpillar shedding its skin

Also, on the bottom of the jar there will be dark-green or black "frass" (their droppings). I usually clean this out every day or so, especially as my critters grow big. If I have many friends on my counter, it can get to be quite "fragrant".

Frass shown at the bottom of the jar

These little creatures eat almost constantly. If you leave during the day, and especially before you go to bed at night, be sure they have a fresh leaf, even two if they are big. They also prefer fresh food, so take out any old leaves and keep your eye on your supply of milkweed leaves. Many nights, I have gone out with a flashlight to pick fresh leaves, because everyone finished their supper before I went to bed!

Tagging Monarchs

One year I decided to participate in the research project at the University of Kansas. They study how Monarchs migrate, where they start, the path they take, and how the weather conditions affect their journey. People all over the United States and Canada sign up to become part of the team. The University sends you all the supplies and instructions. The best part is placing a tiny tag on the wing of each butterfly. Then, the number of the tag, the time, the date, location, wind direction, and weather conditions are recorded for each one released. They have a great website at www.monarchwatch.org.

Luckily, that year was a great year for the Monarchs. I was able to raise about 300 in my laundry room. I did just as I was directed and sent in my information. Later, they sent me the results of the research. Sadly, none of my little friends were found. Even so, that entire summer was a busy and interesting adventure (Also, I did buy a great Monarch T-shirt from them).

From these kinds of research projects, scientists have learned that many Monarchs mass together in Mexico to live in the winter. There are plenty of books written about this great migration, and many other web sites, too.

What was fascinating to me, however, was the fact that Monarchs on the east side of the Rocky Mountains fly very far south, then on to Mexico. They won't go over the Rocky Mountains! Some may even fly only as far as Florida. The Monarchs west of the Rockies will often fly to California, but their flight is a lot shorter than our Connecticut friends. Not fair! The scientists are still working on this mystery of migration.

Don't Be Tricked!

    This is <u>not</u> a Monarch butterfly. It's a Viceroy, but they look very much alike, don't they? These butterflies have a curved line on the hindwings (lower) plus a curved white coloration on the forewings (top). Look at the arrows above. Monarchs are poisonous because its caterpillar eats milkweed, which contains the toxin that makes it poisonous to any insect that eats it. These predators may not die, but will probably get sick, and throw up, just like any sick human might. The trick is this: The Viceroy is <u>not</u> poisonous! Mother Nature is hoping other insects searching for a mid-day snack, have already learned their lesson, and won't be interested in either of these butterflies. It's a protection for both the Monarch and the Viceroy. In the insect kingdom, bright colors often mean "Don't eat me, you'll be sorry!"

Keeping Monarchs for an Extended Time

If you plan to keep your Monarch for more than a day, then you need to read the following:

Monarch butterflies need to have sources of water, carbohydrates, amino acids and salts. It's hard enough to try to copy butterfly food, but a greater challenge is how to get the Monarchs to feed themselves. It is important to keep the food fresh. The easiest food is watermelon, which will keep the butterflies alive for a few days. You can also use a 10% sugar in water solution as your source of nectar (not honey), but these need to be replaced daily. Monarch adults can also be fed using freshly cut flowers or potted plants, but they should be "butterfly" flowers, such as Lantana, Pentas, milkweed flowers, and the butterfly bush. It is best if you can release within a day or so. If the weather is not nice (too cold, less than 60 degrees, or rainy) it is best to postpone their release until the next morning. Please keep them away from your pets and babies, as these are very fragile creatures and need protection, both babies and Monarchs.

Saving the Monarch Butterfly

When I first became interested in these beautiful creatures, I was able to find milkweed everywhere, and there were more caterpillars than I could take care of. Now, milkweed is much harder to find, as are the caterpillars, eggs, and butterflies. Even though the Monarch has not been placed on the endangered list yet, there is such an obvious decline in their numbers that organizations are forming to protect their habitat. I have listed some on page 28 under "Resources", but there are probably more to be found on the internet. I encourage everyone to help in this effort by planting milkweed and butterfly nectar sources on your own property. And yes, Monarch butterflies do have preferences!

Some good annuals are:
-Milkweed
-Cosmos
-Marigolds
-Salvia
-Alyssum
-Heliotrope
-Red Clover
-Sweet William
-Zinnia Biennials
-Queen Anne's Lace
-Nasturtium

Some good perennials are:
-Milkweed
-Bee Balm
-White Clover
-Butterfly Bush (Buddliea)
-Purple Coneflower
-Lupine
-Phlox
-Butterfly Weed
-Coreopsis
-Salvia
-Shasta Daisy
-Yarrow
-Asters
-Thistles
-Hollyhock
-Lavender
-Black-eyed Susan
-Violets

Resources

There are many books and websites about this popular topic. If you are interested in tagging Monarchs, go to www.monarchwatch.org to find out more. This website of the University of Kansas is very informative about all aspects of this subject.

For great pictures, craft ideas, coloring pages, online jigsaw puzzles, lesson plans and more, visit www.kidzone.com and search for "Monarch Butterflies" at the bottom of the home page.

Another great website is www.livemonarch.com. They have a page on "advanced caterpillar and butterfly care". They even have a video of how to repair the wing of a butterfly!

www.YouTube.com has many great videos of every step in the life cycle.

www.Enchantedlearning.com is also a great place to look.

The following are just a few of the books published about Monarch butterflies. However, I have read these and can personally recommend them. Check out www.Amazon.com for many more titles.

Monarchs by Kathryn Lasky

An Extraordinary Life – the Story of a Monarch Butterfly by Laurence Pringle

The Life Cycle of a Butterfly by Bobbie Kalman

Monarch Butterfly by Gail Gibbons

The Moon of the Monarch Butterflies (The Thirteen Moons series) by Jean Craighead George. For older children and adults, a lyrical narrative of the solitary journey of a Monarch Butterfly

Notes

Keep track of your caterpillar and butterfly journey here:

_____

_____

_____

_____

_____

_____

_____

_____

_____

_____

_____

_____

_____

_____

_____

_____

_____